How Big Can You Dream?

by Mark D. Donnelly, PhD.

"A dream is a wish your heart makes."

–Walt Disney

RPSS - Rock Paper Safety Scissors Publishing

Be sure to check out Dr. Donnelly's other Children's books:

- My Name is Rocky
- Theresa's Sock
- Where the Bathwater Goes
- The Worm Doctor
- Last Year When I Was Small
- Twenty-Five Cents
- A Journey for Peace
- Where Did My Wonder Go?
- Sitting Still
- "But I Don't Want to be a Butterfly."
- For Short
- Me - Starting at a new school can be terrifying
- Rory - Imaginary monsters need vacations, too

RPSS - Rock, Paper, Safety Scissors Publishing
429 Englewood Avenue, Kenmore, NY 14223
rpsspublishing.com
publisher@rockpapersafetyscissors.com

978-1-956688-29-0 How big can you dream? - Hardcover

Printed in the USA

RPSS- ROCK PAPER SAFETY SCISSORS PUBLISHING

Recommended for fierce dreamers of all ages.

Good morning, class.
Today, we're going to work on an
exciting new project.

Today, we're going to discuss what inspires you.

I want to discover that special something you'd like to become or dream of doing.

Please dig deep down and use all of your imagination.

I'm curious to see how BIG you can dream.

There are no bad answers.

When you dream about your future, nothing is impossible.

Impossible is just another word for it hasn't happened yet.

Keep in mind, just over a hundred years ago, everyone thought flying was impossible, and nothing would ever replace the horse and buggy.

My dream is to become a Princess, ballerina, artist who carries a briefcase and has an office chair that spins.

I already take dance classes, and I love to draw.

I'm still working on the Princess part.

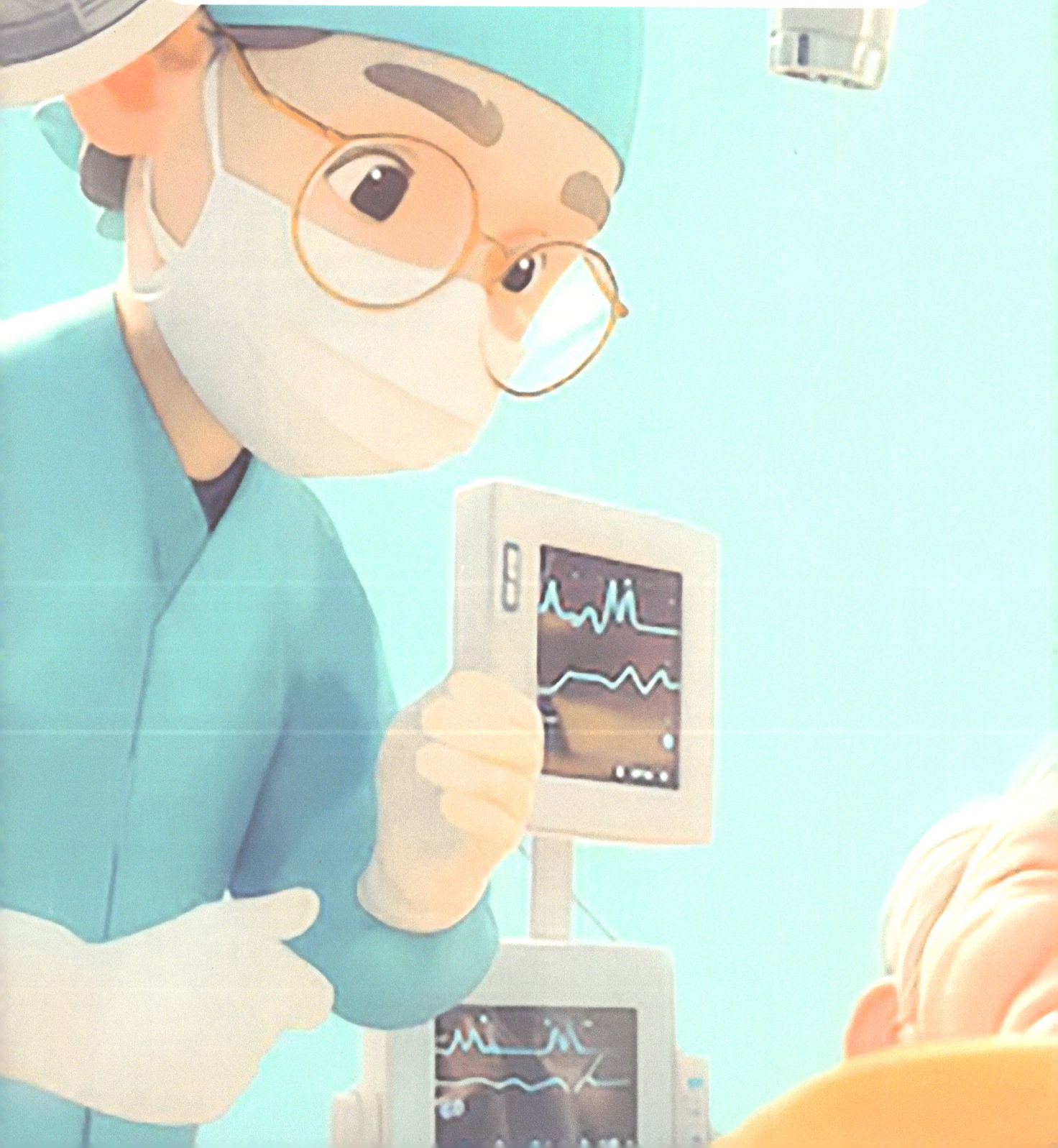

I dream about saving the world, one broken body at a time.

Every night, I dream about becoming an astronaut and going to space.

Someday, I'll visit other planets and explore places that no other person has gone before.

I dream about becoming a writer.

I'd love to have my words inspire others to find great adventures and have wondrous journeys.

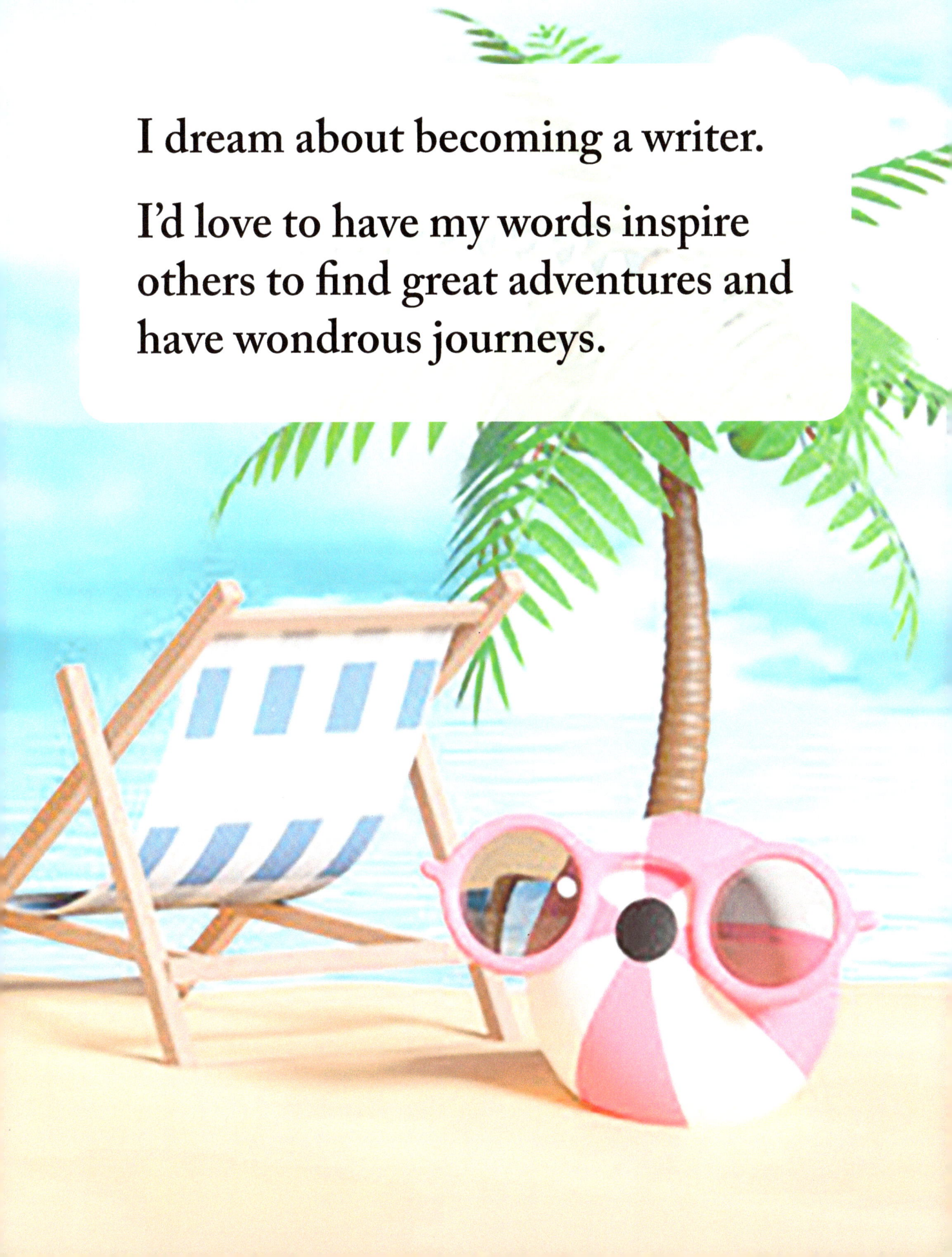

Please don't laugh, but my dream is to play on the Olympic Women's Soccer team.

I'm going to practice hard and be a good teammate.

My dream is to keep children healthy so they can grow up to be their best selves.

My dream is for doctors to find a way to fix my legs so that I can play basketball in the NBA.

I'll jump very high and be incredible at slam-dunking the ball. I want to hit the backboard so hard that it breaks into a million pieces.

I dream about becoming an architect. I want to design solar-powered buildings to help save our environment.

My dream has always been about winning the Indianapolis 500, just like my father and grandfather.

Thank you class for sharing all of your amazing dreams.

The second half of this project is for you to write down how you plan to achieve these goals.

No dream is impossible if you are willing to work hard for it.

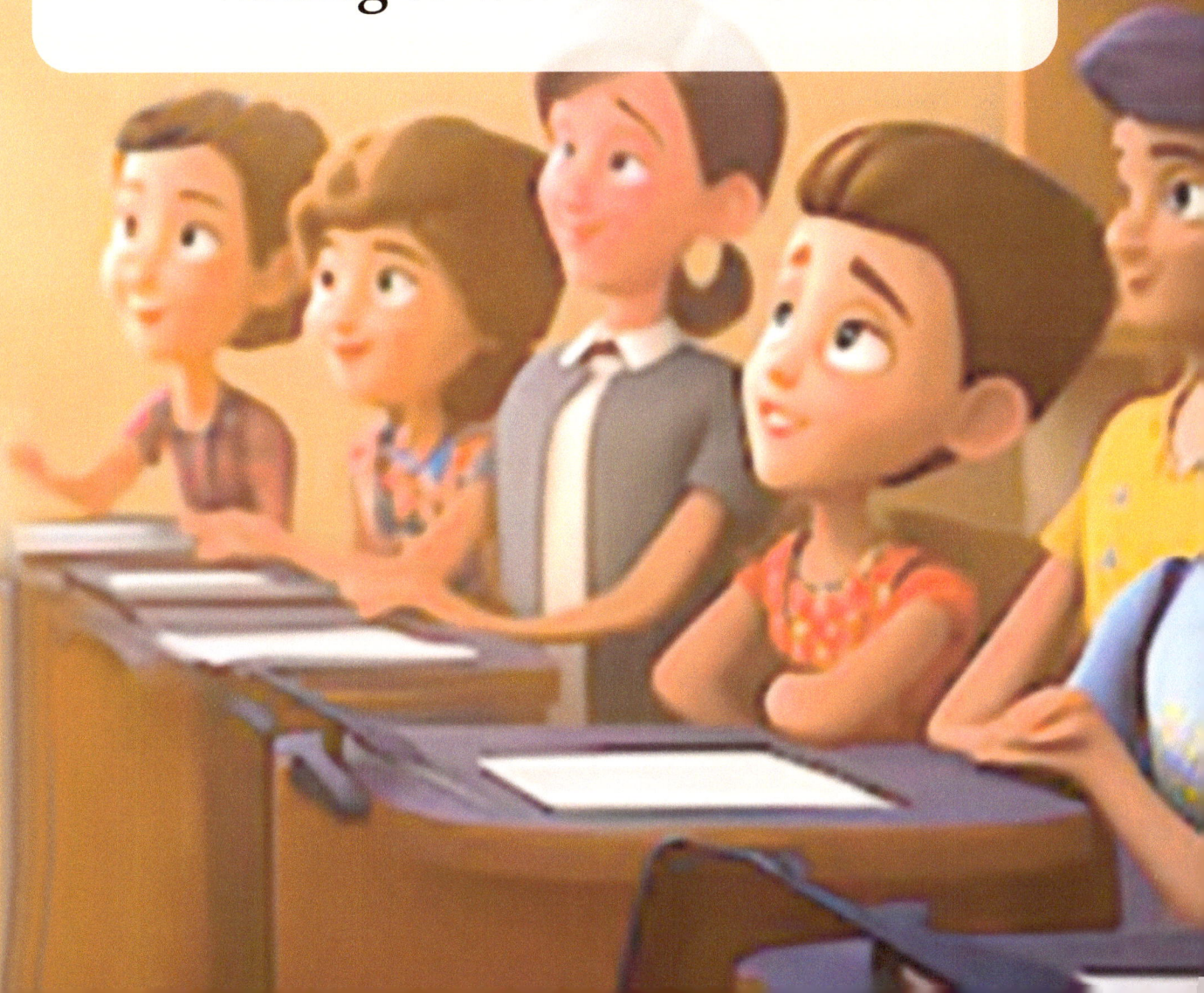

Mrs. Donnelly, now that we've all taken our turns, the class would love to know your big dream.

That's easy. My dream is to see that you will have all the tools you need to make your dreams come true.

That's why I became a teacher.

"All our dreams can come true,
if we have the courage to pursue them."

–Walt Disney

Meet the Author

Mark Donnelly, PhD., is an artist, educator, community activist, Freemason, a proud husband and father of four exceptional children, and a fierce dreamer.

Many believe that the older Dr. Donnelly gets, the younger his imagination becomes.

He is the author of 31 books, including children's titles like *My Name is Rocky, Theresa's Sock, Where the Bathwater Goes, The Worm Doctor, Last Year When I Was Small, Twenty-Five Cents, A Journey for Peace, Where Did My Wonder Go?, Sitting Still, But I don't want to be a butterfly,* and *For Short.*

He has also written about Western New York's history, waterfront, architecture, weather, and a series of novelty cookbooks.

www.ingramcontent.com/pod-product-compliance
Lightning Source LLC
Chambersburg PA
CBHW041549260326
41914CB00016B/1599